WASHINGTON IRVING
Storyteller for a New Nation

World Writers

WASHINGTON IRVING
Storyteller for a New Nation

David R. Collins

MORGAN
REYNOLDS
Incorporated

Greensboro

WASHINGTON IRVING: STORYTELLER FOR A NEW NATION

Picture credits: Library of Congress

Library of Congress Cataloging-in-Publication Data
Collins, David R.
  Washington Irving : storyteller for a new nation / David R. Collins.-- 1st ed.
      p. cm. -- (World writers.)
  Includes bibliographical references and index.
  Summary: A biography of one of America's earliest great literary figures who also
served as a diplomat in Spain.
  ISBN 1-883846-50-1
    1. Irving, Washington, 1783-1859--Juvenile literature. 2. Authors, American--19th
century--Biography--Juvenile literature. [1. Irving, Washington, 1783-1859. 2. Authors,
American.] I. Title. II. Series.

PS2081.C64 2000
818'.209--dc21
[B]

                                                                    99-048295

Printed in the United States of America
First Edition

This book is dedicated to all the writing and teaching colleagues who have enriched my life.

Contents

Chapter One
Problems, Problems 9

Chapter Two
With Pen in Hand 19

Chapter Three
Literary Lion 35

Chapter Four
Living in Europe 52

Chapter Five
A Different Role 67

Chapter Six
Writer and Diplomat 79

Chapter Seven
Sunnyside 90

Major Works 100

Timeline 102

Bibliography 104

Sources 106

Index 110

Washington Irving

Chapter One

Problems, Problems

From the moment the baby entered this world on April 3, 1783, he created a problem. It wasn't that the child was sickly. Every part seemed to be in the right place and in good running order. The baby's lungs were especially powerful as evidenced from the long and loud cries he shared with family and neighbors.

The problem was, stated simply, that his father and mother had run out of names to call their children. William Irving, Sr. and his wife, Sarah, had already welcomed ten children into the world. There were William and Ebenezer, John and Peter, Anne and Catherine and Sarah. Three of the Irving babies had died in infancy, but they also had names before they departed.

"My parents had used up the names of family members and Biblical favorites by the time I arrived," the son recalled much later in life. "Finding a suitable label for me was a challenge."

It was his mother, Sarah, who answered the challenge. The Irving's had lived through the Revolutionary War led by the brave and noble General Washington of Virginia. He was a grand person, a gentleman farmer and soldier of the first order. He was truly the hero of free Americans.

"Let us call the child Washington," Sarah Irving declared. "There is no more respected name in the country. 'Washington Irving.' Yes, it has a fine ring to it."

Finding a larger home became a necessity. Existing elbow-to-elbow was most uncomfortable for the Irving's, and not until they found a former officers' quarters used during the Revolutionary War did they enjoy ample space. The house at 128 William Street was actually two homes, one behind the other with a connecting building between. Sturdily built of brick and lumber, the residence also featured a backyard full of fruit trees whose branches lured the young children to climb them.

William Irving, Sr. was a stern Scottish fellow, a hardware merchant in business with two of his brothers, William and Ebenezer. The family operated business offices in England, too. They kept their store in New York City full of tools, sugar and wine, and thrived on principles promoting much work and little laughter. William Irving, Sr. brought much the same attitude home with him. His children were expected to be quiet and mannered. If they were not, a well-waxed birch rod was kept in the pantry corner for administering punishment.

Young Washington Irving kept a careful eye on the birch rod, hoping to avoid its nasty sting. For the most part, he was successful. His soft voice and poised manners seldom drew his father's attention. In fact, the two barely spoke at all. Now and then, however, his father caught his son drifting off into one of his fantasies. Only then did the rod find its target, while William Irving, Sr. berated his son for being "lazy" and "a scatterbrain."

William Irving, Sr. was not the only person to notice his young son's tendency to daydream. So did Washington's schoolmistress. The four-year-old boy attended Mrs. Ann Kilmaster's classes that she taught at her home, and more than once she caught him gazing out the window. He was always sorry for his inattention, sincerely sorry, but his apology for one misdeed had barely cooled when he was caught again for the same offense.

Washington was certainly not lazy when it came to reading. Even in his youngest years he spent hours in the family library listening to his older brothers and sisters read the works of Shakespeare and Chaucer aloud. The boy might not have understood their meaning, but he enjoyed the language, the words, and phrases. *Pilgrim's Progress* by John Bunyan was his father's favorite, the story of a noble Christian dealing with the struggles of daily life. Every Sunday evening William Irving, Sr. would read from the volume. Thankfully, Sarah Irving livened up the story with her own dramatic interpretations of scenes and question-and-answer sessions. Within the pages of other books, young Washington Irving imagined himself shooting arrows in Sherwood Forest with Robin Hood, sailing on the seas with Sinbad the Sailor, and living on an island with Robinson Crusoe and his companion, Friday. Local newspapers held his interest too, including stories from authors far away whose works were pirated and printed without compensation. It was with the help of authors that Washington Irving escaped the boundaries of old New York City and traveled to different places and times in his mind.

In 1789, Washington Irving got a chance for a real life adventure, right in his home city. The official presidential residence was located in New York City, an ever-growing city of over twenty thousand residents. In April, George Washington came to occupy the executive home as the first president of the United States. Washington Irving's nursemaid, an elderly lady called "Scottish Lizzie," was always on the lookout for the newly chosen leader. The woman thought it would be a grand experience for her young charge Washington to meet the notable hero for whom he was named. Whenever the general got within viewing distance in parades, the woman hoisted the boy into the air for a quick glance at the country's leader.

One day Washington Irving and his devoted nursemaid rounded a corner on Broadway in the business sector of New York City. Who should be entering a shop nearby than the president himself! The nursemaid grabbed the boy's hand and pulled him so fast his feet barely dusted the ground. She slipped into the shop, her eyes seeking out President Washington. Nothing would stand in her way of this opportunity.

Spotting her target in the rear of the shop, the nursemaid bustled forward. A dazed Washington Irving clung to her hand, not knowing what was happening.

"Your excellency," the nursemaid blurted out in front of

Young Washington Irving met his namesake, George Washington, when he was a boy in New York City.

the surprised gentleman. She lifted the brown-haired Washington Irving up into the air. "Here's a bairn that's called after ye!"

Nodding, President Washington laid his hand on Washington Irving's head. "Bless the child," the man said, smiling. It was a moment Washington Irving would never forget.

There were many moments, however, the boy wished he could forget. Family meals were depressing affairs, always begun with lengthy prayers offered by William Irving, Sr., who was a deacon in the Presbyterian church. Although he enjoyed hearing his own words, he expected his children to eat without conversation. Even talk of school was frowned upon.

When young Washington discovered a new set of books in the family library, the boy rejoiced silently. Perhaps one of his uncles had slipped in the volumes, or maybe one of his older brothers. Entitled, *The World Displayed*, the set of books transported Washington to countless foreign countries. Yet the boy did not say a word about the books to his father. The books would have been labeled "useless," without any practical value, appealing only to "scatterbrains" and "dreamers." No doubt the older man would have tracked down the culprit who had brought the volumes into the house, and the birch rod would have claimed another victim.

Washington enjoyed the books so much that he took them to school. While reading one during a study period, he was ordered to remain after class. The schoolmaster demanded to see the volume under investigation. Washington handed it over, expecting to be immediately punished. To his surprise, the boy received praise for his mature reading tastes. Master Benjamin Romaine ran a strict classroom, also administering a birch rod when necessary, but he seemed to recognize a child's need for daydreaming—occasionally.

More praise came to young Washington for his writing skills. Not only was he commended for his clear and distinct script with a quill pen, he also got compliments for the content of his work. "Imaginative" and "creative" were two adjectives he heard often in reference to his efforts.

In the eight years he spent with Master Romaine, Washington flexed his writing talents whenever he could. He wrote poems, trying to describe the seasons and his feelings. He was seldom satisfied with the results. His appreciation for theater led him to write plays. Those, too, left him disappointed. What he most enjoyed was writing essays. A good essay— whether it be about God or human beings, good manners or art, rules of living or philosophy—always attracted readers. It was the sign of an educated man if he could express his opinions well, with clarity and good sense. Washington Irving had no problem writing fine essays.

"You might someday pen a book or two," observed his prophetic schoolmaster. "The writing craft is seldom financially rewarding, yet those who have a way with words often enjoy much respect."

Such words boosted Washington's confidence, but he did not share them at home. He knew his father would have scoffed at such a suggestion. William Irving, Sr. was a practical man. He wanted his children, especially his sons, to waste no time—not one minute. It was fine to enjoy the respect of others, but if it did not contribute to one's financial well being, it was time wasted.

Respecting that thought, Washington Irving decided against attending Columbia College like his other brothers had done. That, to the sixteen-year-old boy, would indeed have been time wasted—and money as well. Instead, he ended his formal education among his peers and selected an individual path. He took a clerk's position with a local law firm. This job offered a chance to study law himself, while being involved with the day-to-day activities of a practicing attorney, Henry Brockholst Livingston.

The decision quickly proved unwise. There was little about law that Washington Irving enjoyed. It was not that there wasn't work to be done. Each day brought clients seeking legal information and rulings regarding land and properties. The Revolutionary War may have achieved freedom for Americans, but it also left countless questions about who owned what—and where—and how much it was worth. Washington Irving serviced each client with a pleasant smile and gentle humor. He offered to look up information or to ask others who would know the answers. Behind that friendly exterior, however, was a depressed and bored soul lacking the "fervent zeal for the correct administration of justice and a disinterested devotion for the law."

Washington's older brother, John, was also studying law. He attempted to bolster his sibling's sagging spirit. "Law is a noble calling," the man said. "You must not let yourself be pulled under by the paperwork. There is much to be said for helping people."

True enough, the law clerk agreed. But Washington did not have the feeling he was helping anyone at all. There was no satisfaction in the work, none at all. It was all "drudgery."

Whenever he could, Washington Irving escaped the dull confines of the law office. One of his friends, James Kirke Paulding, was five years older and had family in nearby Tarrytown. Together the boys visited the old, Dutch village whenever they could. Unlike New York City that was showing new influences in architecture because of other immigrants moving in, Tarrytown was all still Dutch. Each stone house had a steep roof, and each doorway boasted a wooden door that could be opened high or low. When they tired of Tarrytown, Jim and Washington visited another village called Sleepy Hollow. Some folks told of a hired Hessian soldier who had lost his life during the Revolutionary War. In truth, it was his head the soldier lost—and it was said he sometimes rode at night searching for it.

Washington Irving loved hearing such tales. Sometimes he wrote down notes of what he heard. When his brother Peter began editing a daily newspaper called the *Morning Chronicle*, Washington had a chance to share his wisdom and wit to a regular reading audience. On November 15, 1802, the first of a series began appearing. Not wanting to anger or disappoint his father, the nineteen-year-old law clerk called his offerings "The Letters of Jonathan Oldstyle, Gent." His observations about a variety of topics, especially the American theater, won a loyal following of readers.

When an opportunity arose to take a brief vacation from the law office, Washington jumped at the chance. He would have welcomed anything that would have taken him away from the dull office that had become more of a prison cell. Just the thought of not reading a law book or handling a legal document caused Washington's heart to beat faster. It would be grand to visit his married sisters, Ann and Catherine, upstate. He looked forward to sailing on the Hudson River, escaping the sights and sounds of New York City that had become all too familiar.

Chapter Two

With Pen in Hand

From the moment Washington Irving accepted the invitation to visit his older sisters, the law clerk began to pack a traveling trunk. No one had looked forward to a trip with more anticipation. Likewise, no one had ever been more frustrated by the numerous delays encountered by the sloop scheduled to make the voyage. In order to make the trip profitable, the ship's owners wanted a full passenger list and a full hold of trunks and other freight. While this concern for profit frustrated the son, it seemed to be perfectly reasonable to the father. "It's understandable," Washington's father declared. "It is not easy to make a penny these days. It's a wise man who can turn a profit with his business."

Young Washington Irving bit his tongue and held his temper. There was nothing he could say to make his father change his attitudes. To William Irving, Sr., life revolved around how much a man carried in his money pouch and earned each day. The law clerk entertained no such notions. He was sure that his ambition and vision was the right one. As long as a fellow had a pure heart, a full stomach, and a clean set of clothing, he was a rich man indeed. Unfortunately, at this time it seemed that fate sided with the father and the sloop captain. So the frustrated traveler-to-be kept packing and unpacking the family trunk, eager to set sail on the Hudson.

Finally, the day arrived. Washington Irving also carried a journal to record his trip. He might make the journey only once, but he could relive it by reading his accounts again and again.

In New York City, the law clerk had heard people describe the Hudson River waters and surrounding landscape. He had visited the banks of the waterway with his brothers and friends to hunt squirrels. Yet the recollections of other people and his own memories did not even approach what he saw as the sloop slipped through the water. No one had captured the area, its wild and primitive beauty, as Washington Irving had seen it. The Catskill Mountains, "a dismembered branch of the great Appalachian family," held the daily scribbling Irving in awe, as they were:

> seen away to the west of the river, swelling up to a noble height, and lording it over the surrounding country.... Never shall I forget the effect upon me of the first view of them predominating over a wide extent of the country, part wild, woody, and rugged; part softened away into all the graces of cultivation. As we slowly floated along, I lay on the deck and watched them through a long summer's day; undergoing a thousand mutations under the magical ef-

fects of atmosphere, sometimes seeming to approach; at other time to recede; now almost melting into hazy distance, now burnished by the setting sun, until, in the evening, they printed themselves against the glowing sky in the deep purple of an Italian landscape.

So Washington Irving wrote, in words that created pictures, filling the paper with an ever-changing landscape of what he saw. He did not struggle for phrases; they flowed from his quill pen with ease. The journal filled quickly, each page a record of what he had seen, the people he met, and the stories they told. Hours slipped away swiftly as he visited with the villagers. The legends and lore of the area held a special fascination for the New York City visitor. "The whole neighborhood abounds with local tales, haunted spots, and twilight superstitions," he wrote.

Returning to New York City, Washington Irving had made an important decision. Whatever he would do, whether it was law or business or whatever else might call his name as a profession, writing would be a part of his life. It brought a special joy, even exhilaration, to his spirit.

Just as Irving found writing an outlet for positive descriptions and reflections, he could also capture the negative side of living through words. In 1803 he accepted an invitation to accompany Josiah Hoffman, his new legal mentor and Federalist judge, on a trip to Canada. This time, Irving's journal found few cheerful notations. The trip was exhausting and uncomfortable.

"In several parts of the road I have been up to my middle in mud and water," Irving wrote about traveling beside a wagon, "and it was equally bad, if not worse, to attempt to walk in the woods on either side."

Despite the trip's rough conditions, Irving managed to let humor slip into his personal observations. In the eastern part of Canada, his traveling troupe spent a night in a lodge operated by a French woman. The choice was hardly a wise or fortunate decision because both the hostess and her property were extremely dirty. This time Irving not only shared his thoughts in his journal, he scrawled a couple hasty lines above the fireplace:

> Here Sovereign Dirt erects her sable throne,
> The house, the host, the hostess all her own.

Lack of cleanliness in a lodge was mild in comparison to other obstacles encountered on the Canadian trip. As rain beat down on the New York visitors one night, they rejoiced when they spotted a small hut in the wild country. Sadly enough, the one-room structure housed fifteen other wayward travelers, one an ox-team driver who proved to be "the most impudent, chattering, forward scoundrel" Irving had ever met.

"I never passed so dreary a night in my life," the journal keeper wrote. "The rain poured down incessantly, and I was frequently obliged to hold up an umbrella to prevent its beating through the roof on the ladies as they slept. I was awake almost all night, and several times heard the crash of falling trees...and the long dreary howl of a wolf."

Each journal entry reflected the talents of a superb journalist recording the who, what, when, why, and where of the situation. Graphic details and sensual descriptions added style and flavor to the writing. Washington Irving had the instincts of a quality writer. Not only that, he wrote because he wanted to—or felt he had to write.

Whether the trips were enjoyable or disappointing, Irving felt the journals he kept were useful. He reread them often, and was able to relive the events of the past through his daily notes. By contrast, the writings he maintained as a law clerk to Josiah Hoffman brought him no satisfaction at all. If anything, they made him totally depressed. But the clerk continued his studies, largely to please his father. Whenever he could, Irving headed to the New York piers, wistfully watching ships depart for distant ports. The desire to be standing on the decks of those vessels, heading out to sea, grew constantly stronger.

When Washington Irving was twenty-one, his wish came true. Yet it was not in exactly the manner he hoped. Despite a hearty if slightly stocky frame and ruddy skin coloring, he suffered from severe health problems that left him constantly fatigued. A family conference decided that a trip abroad might be the proper prescription. Bidding his brothers farewell proved especially difficult, but within a few weeks, Irving felt much better.

Washington faced many adventures in Europe. While in

France he was interrogated by authorities. Relations between England and France were tense at the time, and French officials thought Irving might be some kind of spy. Convincing them he was not, Irving continued into Italy only to find his ship stopped by a privateer's craft. The boarding party, armed with cutlasses, stilettos, and pistols was a frightening collection of men as Irving reported in his journal. "Their dark complexions, rough beards, and fierce black eyes scowling under enormous bushy eyebrows, gave a character of the greatest ferocity to their countenance." The behavior of the crew matched their appearance, and they ransacked the American ship looking for money and jewels. When the privateers found Irving's letters of introduction to the Governor of Malta, the America craft was released.

Irving made the most of his trip abroad, visiting with other travelers as well as foreigners. He sampled different foods, toured churches and art galleries, and generally soaked up the European atmosphere. He gave no thoughts to his law studies. By the time he returned to America, his health was good and his spirits were soaring.

Another change had taken place in Washington Irving's life during his trip abroad. Naturally, he had missed his family. Yet he had also missed Matilda Hoffman, the youngest daughter of the lawyer with whom he was studying. Although he was now twenty-two and she was fourteen, such a difference in ages did not pose an obstacle during the early nineteenth century. However, there was definitely a problem in the way of a romantic relationship. Irving's future as a lawyer was

Irving pursued a law career so he could marry Matilda Hoffman.

open to question. It was no secret that he lacked enthusiasm for the profession. But when Josiah Hoffman, eager to welcome his law student into the family as a son-in-law, offered Irving a future partnership in the law firm, matters changed a bit. After all, the Hoffman legal firm was the most prestigious in New York City.

"It is a grand opportunity," brother John Irving noted.

True enough, Washington agreed. But it was not the thought of a partnership that appealed to the law clerk: it was the thought of having Matilda for his wife.

With new gusto, Washington Irving renewed his study of law. In November of 1806 he passed the law examination. Each day he hoped his attitude would change, that suddenly he would find the legal profession exciting, or at least, tolerable. For three full years he hoped. It did not happen.

The times he spent with Matilda, however, offered a special uplift to Irving's life. He followed every rule of courtship to the letter, calling on her regularly and always on time, bringing her small gifts, composing notes of affection. They went to lectures and plays, picnicked with each other's families, exchanged books and discussed them, and enjoyed long walks along the waterfront talking about their future. Whether they attended an event or merely spent time together quietly visiting, the two were clearly in love.

Yet his love for writing was equally intense. In 1807, he joined talents with his brother William and his old friend, James Kirke Paulding. Together they put out a magazine called *Salmagundi*. The periodical delighted New Yorkers

THE LITTLE MAN IN BLACK.

SALMAGUNDI;

OR, THE

WHIM-WHAMS AND OPINIONS

OF

LAUNCELOT LANGSTAFF, ESQ.

AND OTHERS.

In hoc est hoax, cum quiz et jokesez,
Et smokem, toastem, roastem folksez,
Fee, faw, fum.   *Psalmanazar.*
With baked, and broiled, and stewed, and toas'd,
And fried, and boiled, and smoked, and roas'd,
We treat the town.

VOL. II.

NEW-YORK:

PRINTED & PUBLISHED BY D. LONGWORTH,

At the Shakspeare.Gallery.
1808

Irving wrote satirical poetry and prose for the magazine *Salmagundi* with his friend James Kirke Paulding and his brother William.

with a humorous and satirical look at their town—its fashions, politics, travel spots, and theatre. Although salmagundi was actually a salad of chopped meats, oils, greens, and anything else the creator wished to toss in, the publication had a serious intent "to instruct the young, inform the old, correct the town, and castigate the age."

Combining poetry and prose, the writers poked fun at many prominent citizens, puncturing the biggest of egos and reputations. Caught up in their writing, the writers failed to copyright their magazine. Their publisher, David Longworth, had a better head for business. He registered *Salmagundi* in his own name and took in most of the profits earned from its twenty issues. *Salmagundi* was published for one year.

Despite this setback Irving felt that his life was finally going in the direction he wanted. Tasting success as a writer, he broke away from some of the conservative elements of his earlier lifestyle. Stylish waistcoats, ties, and breeches now adorned his five foot seven inch frame. He wore his hair a bit longer, hoping to take away attention from a longish nose. His large, dark eyes were always alert, taking in the world and people around him. Cigars became regular companions, one often being puffed on with one hand, while a glass of champagne occupied the other. The jokes he told became more risque, however his writing retained a light and cheerful flavor. Once he had taken Matilda home for the evening, Irving welcomed the company of other business and professional men for another drink or two. Like other single gentlemen who enjoyed the lively conversation in the early morning

The popular Washington Irving was known for his wit, humor, and fashionable dress.

hours, the witty Irving was labeled a "jolly wag of the town." Other than his continued dislike for law, Irving enjoyed the life he led.

Sometimes the hated practice of law did present him with an opportunity for adventure. He was offered a chance to be present at the most exciting trial of the young republic's history. A former vice president was on trial for treason.

Aaron Burr's career had reached its peak when he almost defeated Thomas Jefferson in the 1800 race for president. After the election was decided in the House of Representatives in Jefferson's favor, Burr was sworn in to the second highest office in the land. (In those days the second highest vote getter was automatically elected vice president.)

In 1804 Burr fought a duel with Alexander Hamilton, the former Secretary of the Treasury. After Hamilton was killed, Burr resigned his office and headed for the western frontier along the Mississippi River.

Burr had not disappeared, however, and in 1807 he was arrested for treason. The U.S. government claimed that Burr had tried to create his own country in the west. His goal was to be a dictator or an emperor, just like Napoleon across the ocean in France.

President Jefferson was determined that Burr would pay. The president hated the man who had almost denied him the presidency. He pressured for an early trial and a quick conviction. Irving was hired by friends of the former vice president to offer legal advice to the attorneys trying to free Burr.

Irving spent two months in the capital of Virginia. He wrote

When Aaron Burr was tried for treason in Richmond, Virginia, in 1807, Washington Irving served as one of his legal advisors.

home that he was "absolutely enchanted with Richmond, and like it more and more every day. The society is polished, sociable, and extremely hospitable, and there is a great variety of distinguished characters assembled on this occasion, which gives a strong degree of interest to passing incidents."

The trial was the most popular event of its time. The entire country waited with bated breath to see what would be the fate of the handsome, and little, Aaron Burr. His enemies were quick to judge him guilty—and they savored the notion of making his pay for his crimes with his life. One newspaper writer wrote: "May his treachery to his country exalt him to the scaffold, and hemp [i.e. rope] be his escort to the republic of dust and ashes."

Irving was amazed at how calm Burr appeared. How could a man facing what seemed to be almost certain death and disgrace remain so quiet and dignified. "Burr retains his serenity and self-possession unshaken, and wears the same aspect in all times and situations," Irving wrote. He could not help but feel sympathy for the prisoner held outside of the town, on one of Richmond's seven hills.

The trial was presided over by the Chief Justice of the United States, John Marshall, who was no friend to President Jefferson. The two men differed on most political issues and did not like one another personally. This was one advantage Burr had and he decided to use it. He rose in the trial, where he was working on his own defense, and asked the Chief Justice to subpeona President Jefferson.

Burr's boldness made an impression on Irving. He decided

that "treason was never intended by Burr." He felt that the trial "had assumed the shape of a political persecution." He wanted Burr to go free.

After a dramatic trial in which Burr's cross-examination of James Wilkinson, the most damaging witness against him, proved that his accuser was a liar, Burr was found not guilty. Most of Richmond celebrated. The dashing New York native had won their hearts.

Irving was not in Richmond when Burr was acquited. William Irving, Sr. had become ill. Despite his father's strict rules and harsh manner while Washington was growing up, the son hurried home to help. The older Irving had mellowed in his later years. Before he died, a warm bond developed between the two men. Washington promised his brothers and sisters that he would look after his mother. "I really think it would disturb her too much to have to move," he told them. "She's been in this house so long."

By the winter of 1808, Washington Irving and Matilda Hoffman were officially engaged and making definite plans for their marriage. With his new wife, Irving was convinced he could overcome his negative feelings about the legal profession. Always cheerful, Matilda could make Washington laugh when he least wished.

Yet in February of 1809, Matilda became ill of consumption. Always delicate, she fought to regain her strength. Each day Washington came to her home, sitting for hours beside her bed. With each passing week, Matilda's health declined. On April 26, 1809, the seventeen-year-old girl died with Irving by her side.

Washington Irving was grief stricken. Life without his beloved Matilda seemed impossible. His work offered no comfort; for three years he had continued studying law because she was the reward for his suffering. Now she was gone. For Washington Irving, the road ahead was dark and uncertain.

Chapter Three

Literary Lion

The death of Matilda Hoffman left Washington Irving a broken man. For years he had thought about their future together. All the plans were over now. She was gone. Fifteen years later, Irving wrote about that tragic parting.

"She died in the flower of her youth and of mine but she has lived for me ever since in all woman kind. I see her in their eyes—and it is the remembrance of her that has given a tender interest in my eyes to every thing that bears the name of woman."

Yet Matilda Hoffman's death ended more than a loving relationship. No longer did Irving feel the need to become a lawyer. Matilda was the reason for doing that. Now that reason no longer existed.

At this low point in his life, Washington Irving turned to his writing. It had always given him pleasure and joy. Hopefully, now that he would not be a lawyer anymore, it would also offer him financial security.

There was no need to begin a new literary effort. He had worked with his brother Peter on a manuscript before the older

Irving had gone off to work in the family business offices of P. Irving and Company in England. The book was a humorous takeoff on a popular handbook depicting New York's scenes and sights. Irving enjoyed fooling readers by using fictitious names and making imaginary situations sound totally true. In this case, he created the name Diedrich Knickerbocker, and called the book *A History of New York from the Beginning of the World to the End of the Dutch Dynasty.* The supposed narrator of the chronicle, Master Knickerbocker, traced the story of the "New Netherlands" colony. Attempts to lift his ancestors to places of heroic honor fail miserably for Master Knickerbocker, and the Dutch characters emerge as bungling and inept. In addition, rather than being portrayed as coming to the New World in search of freedom and justice, the settlers from across the Atlantic appear as land and money grubbers.

Irving's plan for promoting the book before its release was almost as elaborate as the content itself. On October 26, 1809, an announcement appeared in the *New York Evening Post* that noted the disappearance of "a small elderly gentleman, dressed in an old black coat and cocked hat, by the name of Knickerbocker." This was the way Irving baited readers' curiosity. On November 6, eleven days later, a second notice appeared in the newspaper, this one in the form of a letter to the editor of the *Evening Post*:

> SIR,
> Having read in your paper of the 26th October last,
> a paragraph respecting an old gentleman by the name

Diedrich Knickerbocker was the alleged author of Irving's *A History of New York.*

of Knickerbocker, who was missing from his lodg-
ings; if it would be any relief to his friends, or furnish
them with any clue to discover where he is, you may
inform them that a person answering the description
given, was seen by the passengers of the Albany
stage, early in the morning, about four or five weeks
ago since, resting himself by the side of the road, a
little above King's Bridge.

He had in his hand a small bundle, tied in a red
bandanna handkerchief; he appeared to be travelling
northward, and was very much fatigued and exhausted.

Curiosity swelled among the newspaper readers. Was the
story true? People stopped by the *Post* offices, some folks
even offering names of whoever the missing person might be.

Ten days later came another article, this one from Seth
Handaside, Master Knickerbocker's landlord. It seemed a
"very curious kind of written book" had been left behind by
the missing man, and if it were not claimed immediately, it
would be sold to pay off Master Knickerbocker's unpaid bill.
With this announcement, Irving dangled the bait a final time.

On November 28, Irving announced the publication of *A
History of New York*, "to discharge certain debts Deidrich
Knickenbocker has left behind." Eager customers hurried to
buy the book. Irving's carefully planned promotion had suc-
ceeded brilliantly. The response to the book's content was
overwhelmingly favorable, excluding those among the Dutch
community who took exception to the author's portrayal of

their ancestors. Although Irving's book did not contain his name at all as the author, his style was unmistakable.

One of the book's most noteworthy fans was the British novelist Sir Walter Scott. "I beg you to accept my best thanks for the uncommon degree of entertainment which I have received from the most excellent jocose history of New York," Scott wrote to Irving. "I have been employed these few evenings in reading it aloud to Mrs. Scott and two ladies who are our guests, and our sides have been absolutely sore with laughter."

Irving was eager to thank Scott personally for his kind remarks. As a new "celebrity" author, Irving also wanted to show his brother Peter what had become of the manuscript they had started together.

But relationships between America and England suddenly soured. American officials accused the English of attempting to stir up the Native Americans in the West, as well as intruding upon American ships at sea. The French were involved too. Since the Irving family business depended largely on imports from England, a blockade of goods coming into New York City proved disastrous. The Irving family coffers dried up.

While studying law and writing, Washington never became active in the family business. He stayed in the background, offering advice and financial help as needed. When the family asked that he visit Washington, D. C., the new capital, and talk to government officials about the business, Irving agreed.

While in Washington, Irving accomplished more for himself than he could for his family. He accepted a job editing a Philadelphia-based magazine called the *Analectic*. He had declined previous editorial positions, but this one allowed him to do more writing.

Busy with writing and editing, Irving paid little attention to the American-British conflict. However, in August of 1814, when the British attacked Washington, D. C. and burned half the city to the ground, Irving was outraged. He immediately joined the New York State Militia and was named a colonel. As aide-de-camp to Governor Daniel Tompkins of New York, Irving saw little action and resigned his position as the war was ending late in 1814.

As a writer and editor of the *Analectic*, Washington Irving helped build the subscriber list. Yet those in charge of the financial end of the magazine lacked his talents, and the publication failed early in 1815.

Finally, in May of 1815, Washington Irving embarked on his long postponed journey to England. On his arrival in Liverpool, he was shocked at what he found. Not only was the Irving family business office in financial depression, his brother Peter was seriously ill. Quick action was called for. Irving took Peter to a care center in Birmingham, and then surrounded himself with the papers and ledgers of P. Irving and Company. It was depressing work, almost as bad as studying law.

"I have never passed so anxious a time in my life," Irving wrote to a friend back in America. "My rest has been broken, and my health and spirits almost prostrated...now that I find myself detained in Europe by unexpected employment, I often feel my heart yearning towards New York, and the dear circle of friends I have left there."

Month after month, in sunlight and candlelight, Irving worked at the family offices. He detested numbers, the endless debits and credits and balances and statements of receipt. They were far removed from the words he loved so much. Now and then he piled forms he had completed working with outside and took fiendish delight setting the papers on fire. Peter's return to work boosted his spirits a bit, but Washington longed for freedom from confinement. He also worried about his mother back home.

Finally, Irving escaped to London to help prepare a new edition of the Knickerbocker history. The book had won fans on both sides of the ocean. What profits he had made, Irving quietly slipped into the family accounts.

Then news of his mother's death reached Washington Irving, and he plunged into depression. His father's stern demeanor had always been balanced by his mother's soft and gentle nature. Now she, too, was gone—and he had not been there during her final illness.

Irving took his grief into the countryside where he joined his sister Sarah and her husband. The change of scenery proved uplifting. They spent hours recalling memories from America, especially reliving the happy and fun times. Irving's trip up the Hudson River was a high point of their conversations. Irving told them about the sights and sounds of the excursion, along with his recollections of the countryfolk. With his gift for storytelling, people in Irving's life became characters, places became settings, tales became plots. The work at the business office had dulled his imagination. Now his mind grew crowded with fresh story ideas, and he took pen to paper, recapturing past facts with fanciful fiction.

The desire to visit Sir Walter Scott grew stronger. "One knows much about a writer through his writings," Irving observed. "I am convinced that we are of like spirits and character."

Irving's observations proved accurate. Sir Walter Scott, the famous Scottish poet, welcomed his American visitor to his home in Abbotsford, Scotland. Irving was then thirty-four years old, and Scott, twelve years his senior. A planned afternoon visit turned into a four-day stay with the two writers spending hours discussing their own ideas as well as the works of other wordsmiths.

Irving's visit with Scott provided him with new enthusiasm and energy. When he returned to his sister's home, he discovered the survival of P. Irving and Company was hopeless. Debts greatly outweighed the assets. Ordinarily, the failure of the Irving business enterprises and the subsequent declaration of bankruptcy might have plunged Washington into great despair. This time, however, there was no time for such feelings. Having sunk his finances into family concerns, he was broke. Writing was a necessity. Inspired and motivated from his visit with Sir Walter Scott, Irving started to shape a collection of short stories based on the folktales he had heard in upstate New York.

Sir Walter Scott was a fan of Irving's *A History of New York*. In 1815, the writers visited at Scott's home in Abbotsford, Scotland.

Irving called his collection *The Sketch-Book of Geoffrey Crayon, Gent.* As usual, he chose to use a pseudonym. If any literary work were judged, Irving felt it should be evaluated on the quality of its content not on the name of its author. It had been ten years since the Knickerbocker history book. Irving was not certain he could still please a reading audience. His introduction reflected that uncertainty: "The following writings are published on experiment; should they please they may be followed by others."

Six short essays appeared in *The Sketch Book of Geoffrey Crayon, Gent.* He wrote of his love of traveling. "How wistfully would I wander about the pier-heads in fine weather, and watch the parting ships, bound to different climes..." Irving also wrote of his passion for reading about voyages. In a selection called "The Wife," his love for Matilda came forth clearly, although she was not mentioned by name.

But it was the folk tales that revealed Irving as a gifted storyteller. The Catskill Mountains had left their mark in Irving's memory. In their shadows, he shared an unusual tale of Rip van Winkle, "a simple good-natured man; he was, moreover, a kind neighbor, and an obedient henpecked husband." Wanting no part of work, Rip loved visiting with friends and wandering around with his dog, Wolf, and a gun. Meeting up with an unusual dwarf, (actually the spirit of old Henry Hudson himself) the lazy Rip is drawn into a drinking party and a game of ninepins, an ancestor of bowling. Too much drink sent him into a very long sleep. When Rip woke up twenty years later, he and his world had changed. He went

Rip van Winkle had the unfortunate experience of sleeping through the Revolutionary War.

to live with his now married daughter and became a favored citizen of his village.

While Irving's story of Rip van Winkle provided an unusual character and plot, another story in the collection emphasized an eerie setting and mood. "The Legend of Sleepy Hollow" blended the author's recollections of the Hudson River Valley with mystery, fun, and fantasy. Irving's description of a superstitious and inept schoolmaster, Ichabod Crane, brought a quick smile to many readers' faces.

> He was tall, but exceedingly lank, with narrow shoulders, long arms and legs, hands that dangled a mile out of his sleeves, feet that might have served as shovels, and his whole frame loosely hung together. His head was small, and flat at top, with huge ears, large green grassy eyes, and a long snipe nose, so that it looked like a weathercock perched upon his spindle neck to tell which way the wind blew. To see him striding along the profile of a hill on a windy day, with his clothes bagging and fluttering about him, one might have mistaken him for the genius of famine descending upon the earth, or some scarecrow eloped from a cornfield.

Irving tells of Ichabod Crane's romance with Katrina Van Tassel, the daughter of a rich Dutch farmer. While the reader is amused by Ichabod's clumsy efforts in the courting department, he later shares a wild encounter with the Headless

The chase between the eerie Headless Horseman and awkward Ichabod Crane has entertained generations of American readers.

Horseman, who supposedly haunted the region of Westchester around Tarrytown.

The Sketch-Book of Geoffrey Crayon, Gent. proved Irving to be a master of the short story. In a unique and smooth style all his own, Irving handled characters, setting, plot, and mood with deftness and surety. The tales won immediate public and critical acclaim in America, where they were published in seven installments beginning in 1819. The book appeared in England in February of 1820.

"It would appear that America now has its first literary lion," declared noted English critic Francis Jeffrey of the *Edinburgh Review*. "Washington Irving writes with imagination, rich and lively. It is refreshing to find a writer from across the sea who is so readable. Let us hope this lion roars with frequency and continued excellence."

Irving, for the first time feeling confident as a writer, was convinced that he could make a living with words. But his experience with the Irving business enterprises had taught him valuable lessons about finances. Often, literary efforts were pirated from one country to another, usually from England to America, the authors receiving no compensation. Irving's background with both law and business made him protective about his literary efforts and allowed him to be paid for his works. Other American writers followed his example.

Although Irving had watched the family business in England sink, the country itself—especially the countryside— had won his heart. He poured out his feelings in a collection of essays entitled *Bracebridge Hall*. In the foreword to the

02

Rip Van Winkle.

a posthumous writing of Diedrich Knickerbocker

By Woden, God of Saxons,
From whence comes Wensday, that is Wodensday,
Truth is a thing that ever I will keep
Unto thylke day in which I creep into
My sepulchre —
                                    Cartwright.

———

Whoever has made a voyage up the
Hudson must remember the
Kaalskill mountains. They are a dis-
·membered branch of the great appala-
·chian family, and are seen away to the
west of the river swelling up to a noble
height and lording it over the surroun-
·ding country. Every change of season
every change of weather, indeed every hour
of the day produces some change in the
magical hues and shapes of these moun-
·tains, and they are regarded by all the

The Sketch-Book of Geoffrey Crayon, Gent. gained Washington Irving the noteriety of a great storyteller.

book, Irving shared his personal impressions of how he was initially regarded in the country: "I was looked upon as something new and strange in literature; a kind of demi-savage, with a feather in his hand instead of one on his head; and there was a curiosity to hear what such a being had to say about civilized society."

English readers liked what this "demi-savage" had to say and the way he said it. The United States was still a new country, and there were people in England whose bitterness over the Revolution still existed. But Washington Irving's talent with a quill and inkbottle mellowed many people's feelings. There was nothing at all "savage" about his literary efforts. He could write, and write well.

In the midst of enjoying the respect of English readers, Irving received sad news from America. His oldest brother, William, was dead. Washington mourned the loss, made all the more dismal by his absence.

While suffering depression from William's death, physical problems settled in too. Despite his enjoyment of England as a country overall, he had never grown accustomed to the rain and dampness. Peter, too, endured regular aches and pains. For Washington, it was his ankles. They became stiff and swollen. Sometimes he could only stand for a few seconds. Doctors suggested a change of climate might be healthy.

Irving's new friend, Sir Walter Scott, had a suggestion. Much of the impressive Crayon volume was based on the legends of America's Hudson Valley region. If Irving could do so much with his homeland as a topic, why couldn't he write stories from other countries, as well? Germany lacked quality literary folklore. Why not draw upon its rich history and sparse literary background for some fresh material?

Irving took Scott's suggestion. The city of Dresden offered much as a writing haven. While he collected material for his next book, Irving studied German, visited art galleries, and wrote plays for the court of King Frederick Augustus I. The pain in his ankles subsided. "I feel the value of life and health now in a degree that I never did before," Irving wrote. "I have always looked upon myself as a useless being, whose existence was of little moment. I now think, if I live and enjoy my health, I may be of some use to those who are most dear to me." Once again, the days were good for Washington Irving.

Chapter Four

Living in Europe

With his body stronger, Irving decided to travel and to try to enjoy as much of the beautiful German countryside as he could. As he sailed along the Rhine River, his thoughts again floated back to the Hudson River in America. But unlike the forests of New York, along the Rhine there were grand castles and convents dotting the German hillsides. He visited Frankfort, Munich and Salzburg—and every small village he could find. As much as he enjoyed his daylight travels, he eagerly looked forward to the night when his quill pen flew across the pages, sharing highlights of the day's adventures. His room was small in size but full of inspiration for a writer—and inexpensive, as well.

"In Dresden I have a very neat, comfortable, and prettily furnished apartment on the first floor of a hotel," he wrote to a friend. "It consists of a cabinet with a bed in it, and a cheerful sitting room that looks on the finest square. I am offered this apartment for the winter at the rate of thirty-six shillings a month. Would to heaven I could get such quarters in London for anything like that money."

Irving's social life was also inexpensive. As an established writer, he was freely welcomed into Dresden's finest homes, the guest of honor at many dinner parties. He enjoyed the attention. As he slipped into his forties, extra pounds settled onto his middle, his hair thinned a bit, and traces of a second chin appeared. The life of a visiting celebrity took its toll. But the sore ankles were gone, and his step was quick and lively. He proved quite able on a ballroom floor, and his polished manners were always on display with every dancing partner.

Irving attracted the attention of more than one young lady in the Dresden social circle. Yet Emily Foster was special. Only eighteen, she lived with her mother and sister, Flora, in part of a palace. Like Matilda Hoffman, Emily possessed a quick wit and a cheerful disposition. Washington Irving was in love again.

His feelings for Emily brought Irving to the Foster residence every day. Together they wrote plays which were presented in a small theater within the palace. Tom Thumb and King Arthur proved big crowd pleasers.

The Foster family unexpectedly left for their native England, leaving Irving confused and disappointed. Despite all of his writing, Irving never chose to put in words what had caused the end to the romance.

Dresden no longer had the same appeal to Irving. He headed to Paris where he took rooms at 83 Rue Richelieu. His brother Peter came from England and became a welcome roommate.

Carefully Irving scoured his notes about Germany. Each

told its own little story, like the tales recorded from Salzburg: "There are little men and women that live in the interior of the mountains," he wrote, "and sometimes visit the Cathedral of Salzburg. There is a hole in the foundation, leading to water, through which is said they enter. They say the Cathedral was built upon what was once a lake."

Irving had collected information about gnomes and pixies from deep woods, inside tall mountains, and along snaking rivers. He had gathered research from old German scribes— tales of ancient castles and fortresses, and of battles and battlefields. His notebooks took shape and gradually became the manuscript, *Tales of a Traveler*, appearing in 1824.

The reaction to Irving's new book was immediate. The critics found it disappointing, even dull. Some claimed it was filled with lies and silly fables. "Let us hope that this traveler does not visit us again," wrote one German book reviewer. "If he does, let us hope he leaves his writing tools at home. The legends and lore of this country deserve far better than is found on these pages."

Irving was devastated at his book's reception. One moment he had felt he was a gifted writer. The next he was criticized by the very audience he so badly wanted to please. After thinking about the reviews, he thought that he understood why the British critics had been so harsh. "I have kept myself so aloof from all clanship in literature that I have no allies among the scribblers for the periodical press; and some of them have taken a pique against me for not having treated them a little more cavalierly in my writings." But the sharp attacks and

Emily Foster (right) and her sister Flora (left) enjoyed Irving's company while their family lived in Dresden, Germany.

criticism from the United States hit him more deeply.

For days he stayed inside his Paris apartment, not wanting to see or talk to anyone. Peter coaxed his brother to eat. Irving had no appetite. Nor could he sleep.

"I may have been a writer once," Irving wrote to a friend. "That is behind me. I shall do my readers the kindness of setting my quill down and closing my inkwell forever."

The festive atmosphere of Paris annoyed the brooding author. He stopped going to the cafés and bright nightspots that had once been his daily eating and drinking places. For a time he became a recluse, choosing to avoid any contact with people. The weeks slipped slowly into months, the months into years. By 1826, Irving knew he had to break away from the dreary life he'd been living. His brother Peter encouraged a change in scenery, and this time the two headed to Spain.

The "stern, melancholy country, with rugged mountains, and long sweeping plains, destitute of trees" matched the mood of Washington Irving. Much like Spain, he felt "silent and lonesome," as he would write later. He wanted to go unnoticed by people, to escape the past life he had led.

But Alexander Everett, the head of the American legation in Madrid, had other plans for Irving. He requested the writer translate Martin Fernandez de Navarrete's recently published collection of documents pertaining to the voyages of Christopher Columbus. Irving protested that he did not know Spanish well enough to take on such a task.

"It is said you learned German quickly and fluently when you lived there," Everett fired back. "And your French, I am told, is flawless. Hopefully, you have not forgotten your native tongue."

Irving was amused. Yes, he still knew English. But the writer was still uncertain about his ability to translate. Peter offered to help any way he could. The two brothers, both now confirmed bachelors, had become very close. Irving agreed to try the Columbus project.

Foreign languages did come easily to the American writer, and Irving enjoyed visiting the Spanish libraries and archives. He wanted to be faithful to de Navarrete's work, and make sure every Spanish word matched its English translation.

A visit to Granada in the south of Spain added to his appreciation for the country. Irving remembered reading about the kingdom and last stronghold of the Moors in the books that had appeared mysteriously in the family library when he was a child. The Moors from North Africa had ruled Spain for more than nine centuries until the Catholic monarchs, King Ferdinand and Queen Isabella, came to power in 1492. To Irving, Granada had been a faraway place described in a book. Now, he could finally see the city, full of people and places to be explored.

But to do the work on the Columbus manuscript required Irving to live in Madrid. The American Consul, Obadiah Rich, had a huge collection of reference books, many of them old Spanish documents about America. He even invited Washington and Peter to stay in the counsulate building during the project. The brothers agreed.

Despite Irving's newfound interest in Spain, memories of

old New York and the Hudson River persisted. To an American friend, Irving wrote:

> There is charm about that little spot of earth; that beautiful city and its environs, that has a perfect spell over my imagination. The bay, the rivers and their wild and woody shores, the haunts of my childhood, both on land and water, absolutely have a witchery over my mind. I thank God for my having been born in so beautiful a place among such beautiful scenery; I am convinced I owe a vast deal of what is good and pleasant in my nature to the circumstances.

Irving's desire to return to the United States arose often in the winter of 1825-26. But the work on the Columbus manuscript demanded his focus. Peter, however, was always ready to persuade his brother to take an excursion. Naturally, Washington kept notes.

"Breakfast. coffee and milk excellent bread. Drive all day thro a wild mountainous country with a stream running thro —villages of rugged looking houses—Men with sashes...pass mount of Bergara—just before alighting to walk it we stop at mountain inn in small village—mules with bells..."

Irving's travels continued to brighten his spirits. The negative reviews of the Germany book and the romance with Emily Foster faded as the sightseeing continued.

"arrive for the night at hotel at village of Lerma—great stable full of mules and horses. *Kitchen* fireplace on a raised

Obadiah Rich, the American Consul, offered Irving and his brother Peter lodging in the consulate building while they visited Madrid.

platform of Brick...in center of the room. A huge funnel about it for chimney—benches round it where travelers sit—lamp hangs hitchd to a cord—half a kid turning on spit..."

Washington Irving filled notebook after notebook with his observations. But the Columbus project ran into trouble. The book by de Navarrete was filled with quotes. To stay true to the original text would be filling pages with boring content. Irving proposed a new idea to Alexander Everett. The writer suggested a book about the explorer himself, a full biography, using all the documents in the text. Everett thought it was a fine idea.

Irving took to the assignment with renewed zest. He got up at five o'clock each morning and spent the next twelve hours at his desk. Hour after hour, Irving read and wrote. He even ate his meals while editing his text. He had never worked so hard. Some days he produced up to twenty pages of usable manuscript.

"I am caught up totally in the work I am doing," Irving wrote his sister Sarah in England. "This is what I was meant to do, to put words on paper."

Peter insisted his brother relax during the evening. One night they dined with friends, where Washington Irving met a painter named Sir David Wilkie. When the Scotsman suggested doing Irving's portrait, he was flattered and agreed.

Wilkie introduced Irving to another of Madrid's spectacles. Bullfighting brought out the city's crowds wearing their most colorful costumes. The people poured into the round stadium. Bands played while everyone cheered. Rousing

Irving began a biography of Christopher Columbus after translating a collection of original documents about the explorer.

cheers went up when the bullfighters entered the arena. Their satin breeches, sashes, and jackets shone in the afternoon sun. Over their arms, the men carried red flags to lure the bulls, who were confined in dark stalls until their release, one at a time, into the arena. They snorted loudly, pawing the ground. Then a gate went up. The first thing the bull saw was a red flag. The people cheered as the animal lunged toward the bullfighter. The blades of the swords glittered in the sunlight. As each weapon plunged into the bull, a wave of wild cheers deafened the arena.

Irving recoiled at the sounds and the sights of the arena. Wilkie encouraged his guest to go again. Then, perhaps, the sport would become more appealing. But the writer wanted no part of what he determined to be "a barbarous spectacle." Irving preferred watching Rickett's Circus with its trick and fancy riding stunts. There was no bloodshed in that sport.

Knowing that the Columbus biography would run more than one volume, Irving resolved not to hurry his work. Spanish officials were so interested in Irving's projects that they furnished him with assistants. The writing came easier with others helping with the research. Even before he had finished the Columbus manuscript, Irving's next book project took form. He sought to trace the entire history of Spain, including all of the monarchs, and how they had changed the country. Whenever he chose to break away from the Columbus manuscript, he worked on an outline of Spanish history.

Immersed in his work, Irving tried to avoid any distractions. As he sensed the end of the Columbus manuscript, the

Allowing for a visitor while busy at work, Irving met the young Henry Wadsworth Longfellow in Madrid.

biographer gave strict orders not be disturbed. However, he made an exception one day for a nineteen-year-old traveler from the United States. A college graduate, he was in Europe studying languages so that he could return to America and teach. It was the young man's admission that caused Irving to blush.

"I have always admired your work," the student acknowledged. "Your *Sketch Book* is the finest literary effort I've ever come upon. And I felt the critics were far too harsh with your *Tales of a Traveler*. It has such a fine style, such a smooth flow."

Of course, Irving enjoyed every moment he spent with his young visitor. It was exciting to know that his writing might affect the work of future writers. He promised to remember the man's name—Henry Wadsworth Longfellow.

A History of the Life and Voyages of Christopher Columbus ended up running four volumes. It was the first of Irving's works to carry the author's name on the title page. The work won quick praise from both reviewers and the general reading public.

To celebrate the favorable reception of his latest book, Washington suggested to Peter they tour the entire country. But Peter begged off, preferring to return to Paris. David Wilkie agreed to go, as did another friend, Prince Dimitri Dolgorouki, who worked at the Russian Embassy in Madrid.

Irving left Madrid in April of 1828. The air was dry with warm breezes stirring the fig and palm trees. He headed south with a particular destination in mind. High in the Sierra

Nevada was the city of Granada, a collection of white stucco homes with red tile roofs. At the edge of the city was the Alhambra, summer home to the Moorish emperors. This palace-fortress built in the thirteenth century was now in ruins. The bright smooth tiles had been chipped from the walls by gypsies. It's magnificent fountains lay unused and gardens untended. Irving traveled further, and stopped in Seville to write about Granada. Later, David Wiklie joined him there. By October, he had mailed the manuscript about the city to his publisher in New York.

Irving had another idea while in Seville. He wanted to share the story of the Alhambra. In Arabic, *alhambra* means "red." The name comes from the color of the tiles used to build the palace-fortress. The Alhambra was now inhabited by locals, some who claimed a rich heritage of Spainish or Moorish blood. Irving wanted to capture the legends that still lived within the palace walls. When the governor of Granada learned of Irving's intentions, he invited the writer to live in the fortress's royal apartment to do his work. Irving jumped at the chance. It turned out to be a wise choice.

"I am so in love with this apartment," wrote Irving, "that I can hardly force myself from it to make my promenades. I sit by my window until late at night, enjoying the moonlight and listening to the sound of the fountains and the singing of the nightingales."

A caretaker, Doña Antonia Molina, prepared Irving's meals and washed his clothing. Another helper, a young man named Pepe, brought in flowers each day and did any other errands as needed. Only Spanish was spoken inside the fortress walls. Washington Irving was a respected author, and everyone was willing to help him create. It was a perfect place to write.

Chapter Five

A Different Role

As Washington Irving labored over his book about the Alhambra, he did not suspect that government officials in the United States had special plans for him. Foreign diplomacy was still young in the United States. Representatives were selected more on popularity and on their social conections than on their skill in international relations. To many people working in the government, Washington Irving would be a perfect choice as a diplomat. His name as an author was known and respected, he was fluent in four languages, and he possessed impeccable manners and social graces. He was also a lawyer, and this training could prove beneficial to a new ambassador. The big question was whether or not he would accept a government appointment.

When Irving received an invitation to become the Secretary of the American Legation in London, he was surprised. He had never considered himself in such a role. Not only that, he had become terribly fond of Spain. The job in England required serious consideration. Finally, he made his decision.

"As it appeared to be the general wish of my friends that

I should accept this appointment," he wrote to his sister. "I have done so; but I assure you when I took my last look at Alhambra from the mountain road of Granada, I felt like a sailor who has just left a tranquil port to launch upon a stormy and treacherous sea."

His words proved prophetic. Once he arrived at the offices of the American Legation in London, he hoped to finish up the Alhambra manuscript quickly. However, he had not planned on the ambassador to England becoming ill. Because of the ambassador's illness, Irving took on many extra duties.

Washington Irving proved remarkably able in his new post. His greatest strength seemed to be his ability to deal with people. Many were upset about one thing or another when they arrived, yet by the time they left Irving, they had been comforted and well assisted.

"The secret, I believe, is listening to people," the legation secretary wrote to a friend back in the United States. "When a person encounters a difficulty and no one appears to be concerned, that difficulty expands considerably. Sharing a moment's interest in another person's problem often leads to a solution."

Solutions were not always easy to come by. At one dinner party, Irving found the invited guests moving toward an out-and-out confrontation. Although the Revolutionary War had been over for over fifty years, there were still individuals from England and the United States who carried distrust for the opposite side. As often happened, the American ambassador was too ill to attend the gathering. Voices at the dinner table became louder and faces reddened. Irving signaled to the attending servants to cut back on the wine being poured. But finally, he knew the right words were needed to squelch an unpleasant scene. He did not like making speeches, yet there were times when it could not be avoided.

"The matter of who was right and who was wrong seems insignificant at this point in time," Irving observed. "What seems more important is the present and the future. The past is over and done with. Would it not be wise to move on in a manner that benefits both of the two grand nations, the countries and their people?"

It was impossible to challenge the wisdom of Irving's thought. His quick thinking and rationality helped to put the guests at ease.

Irving continued to carry out his duties in London. But by the spring of 1832, he was overcome with the desire to return to the United States. After all, he had been gone from his homeland for seventeen years. On April 1, 1832, a new ambassador arrived from the United States to head the American Legation. Washington Irving turned in his resignation and packed his trunks.

If Washington Irving thought he would slip back to the United States without fanfare, he was mistaken. His family and friends hosted a public dinner at the City Hotel in New York. In the midst of crystal chandeliers and elaborate wall tapestries, the elite of society mingled, wearing their best waistcoats and gowns. Washington Irving was called upon to speak. One thing he wanted to clear up was his personal feelings about America. He knew there were those who wondered why he had remained in Europe so long. Did England, Germany, France, and Spain claim his allegiance? Had he merely returned home for a brief visit?

"I'm asked how long I mean to remain here." Irving said at the dinner in his honor. "They know but little of my heart or my feelings who can ask me this question. I answer, as long as I live."

The writer's words brought deafening shouts and cheers. From pockets and purses came handkerchiefs, waving in the air. Washington Irving was back to stay, and the American public was thrilled to welcome him home.

In 1832 *The Alhambra* appeared, and copies were eagerly bought. Irving's style held his readers until the final page. The public begged for such a volume with an American background. By now, Irving knew the importance of listening to his reading audience. He also knew, geographically, where the future of the nation was headed. The West held America's attention as settlers moved from the East to a new life. The government promised free acres to those who would settle and clear the soil. The future lay westward.

Irving traveled west to explore the expanding country and to find material for an American story. His three companions on this trip were Henry Ellsworth, Charles LaTrobe and the Count de Pourtales, whom he had met returning from Europe. They planned to travel to Fort Gibson on the Arkansas River, and then from there explore the frontier. The four bought passage on steamboats down the Mississippi and Ohio Rivers.

Iriving's enchantment with the Alhambra legends inspired the subject of his eighth book.

On the decks of the vessels, Irving saw "clearings on the banks of the rivers" or "a solitary log hut with corn fields among the forests." Wild ducks played in the glassy waters. The group traveled southwest, stopping in villages and towns, talking to the pioneers headed to no certain location but filled with grand expectations.

Irving and his companions came into contact with Native Americans, too. Most notably were the Cherokees, Osages, and the Kickapoos. Irving sat around blazing campfires, eating venison, and afterwards, listening to the howls of wolves and the hooting of owls. Herds of horses and buffalo thundered as they ran, shaking the earth. He wrote home from Arkansas: "We are now on the borders of the Pawnee country, a region untraversed by white men, except by solitary trappers. We are leading a wild life, depending upon game, such as deer, elk, bear, for food, encamping on the borders of brooks, and sleeping in the open air under trees, with outposts stationed to guard us against any surprise by the Indians."

It was a life Washington Irving had never known, and he took to it like a pioneer who seeks new adventure each day. Irving left Fort Gibson a month later alone and headed home by way of New Orleans. There Irving mingled with Creoles and Spaniards, with plantation owners from Georgia and French fur traders. Irving was impressed by the combination of European and New World influences in the city.

In 1832, Irving compiled an essay, "A Tour on the Prairies," appearing in 1835. He wrote about the raw conditions of the prairie: from fording a stream in a buffalo-hide boat to the chaos within a camp threatened by fire and Native Americans.

After some success with his essay, Irving was contacted by John Jacob Astor, a western developer and long-time friend. Astor commissioned Irving to write his next book. *Astoria* is a graphic account of the establishment of the Pacific Fur Company at its northwestern post at the mouth of the Columbia River. Astor's vision was to build the largest fur trading company in the world. He would set up a string of forts from the Louisiana territory west to the Pacific Ocean. Here, at the mouth of the Columbia River, he built Astoria, the fort that would serve as the North American link to his international shipping business. From Astoria he could ship furs to Chinese ports and then restock his ships with silk and spices destined for the American market.

Irving spent months at Astor's mansion, Hell Gate, during 1835. He asked his nephew, Pierre, to join him and act as his aide, searching through stacks of Astor's intensive diaries and business reords. Irving was determined to make his account of the Pacific Fur Company as accurate as possible. Finally, the manuscript was completed. It traced the events in the northwestern fort for nearly a decade beginning in 1808, and ending with its short ownership by British Canadians after the War of 1812, when it was re-named Fort George.

It's sequel, *The Adventures of Captain Bonneville*, reached the American public in 1837. Irving based this book on the diaries of Benjamin Bonneville, an experienced fur trapper and trader. Captain Bonneville became a government agent who was sent to gather secret information about English and Mexican movements in the West. These lands were not yet states, and both England and Mexico laid claim to parts of them.

Each volume received mixed reviews, but none seemed to capture the sparkle and zest of *The Alhambra* or *The Sketch Book.* Irving knew why. His efforts to share the excitement of the American West lacked the passion that usually guided him. As a writer, his strength lay more in the past, the legends of people and places. Someone else should look into the present and the future. Maybe a younger man could do it better.

Irving decided to rest his pen a bit. There were others matters to attend to, especially with the people he held dear. Whether in the United States or Europe, Irving had not known a home since he was a boy. Always it was boardinghouses, apartments, rooms in a castle or a library. As the guest of honor he was wined and dined. He could not help but envy the warmth of the atmosphere and decor of many of the homes he visited. Often, as he rode his carriage to the home of the host or hostess, or afterwards, when he headed back to his hotel room, Irving longed for a home of his own. Living in Europe had been far less expensive than living in the United States, and Irving had built up a comfortable treasury. He was thrifty, his past activities with both law and business turning him into a practical rather than an extravagant spender. Now, every spare moment he spent searching for a home. One thing was certain—it had to be large enough to accommodate a

John Jacob Astor commissioned Irving to write an account of the Pacific Fur Company.

quantity of nieces and nephews, all who felt their "Uncle Washington" was very special.

Irving found a large, Dutch cottage on the shores of the Hudson River. Two miles south of the rustic town of Tarrytown, New York, the house not only boasted many rooms, it was perfect for adding a few more. Irving did exactly that, and he also added European architectural features that reminded him of his years spent abroad.

"You are welcome to visit me at Sunnyside at any moment, announced or unannounced," Irving told his family and friends. There was little doubt that he planned to continue writing, but it was also obvious that the pen would be laid aside whenever company arrived.

Company did arrive, frequently. A carriage would roll up to the cottage entrance with a smiling niece or maybe a nephew with a new wife on his arm.

Friends came too. Some were literary colleagues, while others were longtime readers and fans. Master Henry Longfellow, who had visited Irving in Spain was especially welcomed. Longfellow's own literary efforts were already winning favor and wide audiences in the United States. Whether family or friend, each visitor was made welcome with giant meals and a warm bed. Irving prided himself on being a hospitable host. He could usually be persuaded to read beside a roaring fire after dinner, always from his own work, of course!

Appreciation for Irving's work grew constantly. The *Southern Literary Messenger* officially named him one of the

Irving's home, Sunnyside, was located on the banks of the Hudson River.

country's five most outstanding authors. Many scoffed at that award, feeling Washington Irving was not *among* the top five writers, he *was* the top one.

"One does not put words to paper to win awards and honors," Irving noted, "but rather to reach the minds and hearts of readers. With that now said, I might also say that I should not turn away any recognition addressed to my humble personage."

Modesty was always a part of Irving's character, despite the fact that he had become one of America's best known citizens. Government officials sought his advice in matters regarding the European countries in which he had lived. Impressed with General William Henry Harrison, Irving officially joined the Whig political party in 1840.

"If one wishes to be an active contributor to the strength and quality of his country, he should be willing to share his ideas and time," Irving declared. Harrison's election as president delighted him.

Irving kept within the confines of Sunnyside, content to entertain any guest who came knocking at his door. Soon, opportunity came knocking. Once again, the life of Washington Irving was about to change.

Chapter Six

Writer and Diplomat

Whenever and wherever Washington Irving traveled he found his books being read. Men and women, young people and older, were eager to share their admiration and appreciation.

Few readers were more impressed with Irving's literary efforts than Daniel Webster, the distinguished senator from Massachusetts. Not only did the statesman enjoy reading Irving's work, he also found the writer an exciting conversationalist.

"We have in our government many who have extensive vocabularies," Webster told Irving one night at a dinner party. "Unfortunately, too many of those individuals feel obliged to display every word they know at every opportunity. You, on the other hand, know the value of the right word at the right time."

Irving was flattered. There were many people who considered Webster the finest orator in the senate, able to sway a colleague's vote with a short speech. Like Irving, Webster was also a Whig. When Webster called upon Irving one afternoon, the host knew the senator had not come for idle conversation.

Webster did not waste time or words getting to the purpose of his visit. He was the new secretary of state in the administration of President William Henry Harrison. Webster asked Irving to accept a governmental post—Envoy Extraordinary and Minister Plenipotentiary to Spain.

Washington Irving requested time to ponder his decision. Life was good at Sunnyside, each day filled with visitors. Irving loved to walk visitors around his grounds, proudly pointing out the different touches he had added to the original Dutch cottage. It was also a pleasure to settle into a carriage for a visit to others. Washington, D. C. was an enjoyable journey where he would be welcomed by senators, ambassadors, or by the president himself.

Now in his fifties , Irving still rejoiced in having children around. His nieces and nephews snatched every chance to spend time at their uncle's home. Nearby woods were filled with berries often ripe for picking and places to hide. Swings hung from sturdy branches and fires in the evening attracted happy singers and storytellers.

But Spain still held a special place in Irving's heart. The years he had spent there brought back wonderful memories of friendly people with colorful clothing and spirited singing, the tall rugged mountains scratching at the skyline, the long plains spread as far as the eyes could see. On the practical side, it had been the least expensive country of all the European nations.

Daniel Webster invited Irving to be the U.S. foreign minister to Spain.

Finally, Irving made up his mind. He would go to Spain. No one was more pleased about the appointment than the Spanish foreign minister in Washington, D. C.

"He is one of the men of greatest reputation, as much in America as in Europe, for the purity and elegance with which he writes the English language, and he has a most favorable opinion of our country, or customs and the character of our people."

Before he left for Spain, Irving was called upon to welcome another renown author to the United States. Always hesitant to make any kind of a formal public speech, Irving tried to decline. Yet when officials hosting a grand banquet welcoming Charles Dickens to the country said that it was only proper that America's greatest author introduce Britain's greatest author, Irving accepted. Personally, Irving considered the noted visitor to be rather short on manners and sloppy in appearance. All his life Irving prided himself on proper decorum and appropriate dress. However, he sensed a kind of duty in his task. When he rose at the head table, nervousness before such an impressive audience chased away the introduction he had planned. In a brave gusto, he declared, "Charles Dickens, guest of the nation!" The applause shook the room.

As for Dickens, his nerves were neatly tucked away for the night. With true affection for his host, the English novelist said, "Everything you have written is upon my shelves, and in my thoughts, and in my heart of hearts."

Irving was taken aback by the praise, nodding with appreciation. When he sailed for Spain aboard the *Independence*

Irving welcomed the well-known British author Charles Dickens to the United States.

on April 10, 1842, he carried Dickens's generous remarks in his coat pocket.

Life abroad had allowed Washington Irving to make many friends in the past. In selecting a staff to serve with him, it was difficult because he knew a variety of people who would perform their duties well. Not only that, there were many people who wanted to serve with him. He was known to be fair, expecting the best from all of his staff but not being a difficult taskmaster. Irving spent time in both London and then Paris, gathering together a well-rounded team of workers. Each staff member had a specialty, whether it be in speaking and translating, or formal diplomacy with visiting dignitaries, or just congenial manners and respectful attitude.

But there was no doubt who was in charge—and who kept the American consuls in Malagna and Barcelona running smoothly. Washington Irving knew the past and present of Spain. His research provided him with a rich background in every phase of the country's culture. Whether he talked to a native Spaniard or a visitor from another country, he offered information with depth and detail. Knickerbocker, Rip van Winkle, Ichabod Crane—the people of Spain knew all of Irving's literary characters because all of his works had been translated. If his American creations endeared him to the Spaniards, the works he had written about their own country placed him high in their esteem. Wherever he traveled, he was recognized and applauded.

Irving's appointment soon called him. In 1842, the country was going through a major political crisis. Twelve-year-old

Queen Isabella II was caught in the midst of the fight for control of the country. The girl's representative was the Regent Baldomero Espartero, a disciplined soldier who had fought against Napoleon in Europe and revolting Spanish colonists in America. Now he was fending off an opposing leader named Ramón María Narváez. Narváez hoped to gain control of the young Isabella and then take control of the country.

Spies lurked in every counsul building. Plotters spoke in whispers, suddenly becoming silent at the approach of a stranger. New faces appeared regularly in the Spanish parliamentary body. Stories were told of kidnappings and murders of government officials. It was not the atmosphere in which Washington Irving liked to work. In one message sent back to Washington, D. C., he compared it to "bargaining at the window of a railroad car; before you get a reply to a proposition, the other party is out of sight."

This atmosphere, with its mystery and intrigue, might have appealed to Irving the writer. But as a diplomat, it held little charm. He recognized Regent Espartero as the leader of the Spanish government and conducted official business with him. Although Irving was known as a "people person," he probably put too much trust in the shrewd and devious dictator. The Spanish leader was constantly claiming that he was the victim of assassination attempts and conspiracies. The naive Irving believed the wildest of tales.

Revolution broke out in Spain in 1843. Many foreign officials having offices in Madrid feared for their lives. Not

Washington Irving. In the daytime he watched from the windows of the American Embassy, keeping his pen alive with descriptions of what he saw, "...all the gates were strongly guarded; the main squares were full of troops, with cannon planted at the entrances of the streets opening into them." He wrote in another letter, "Troops were stationed in the houses along the main streets, to fire upon the enemy from the windows and balconies, should they effect an entrance; and it was resolved to dispute the ground street by street, and to make the last stand in the royal palace...." Irving seemed to be unaware of the potential danger to his own life. After sunset, he roamed the city streets, taking in the fighting and shouting among the people. Cannons sounded at the gates of Madrid; Narváez waited for just the right moment to storm the city and capture Queen Isabella. Washington Irving watched the spectacle like an awestruck child.

Perhaps it was the mental strain that weakened Irving, but by the end of the first year of his service, he was frequently ill. He was expected to send regular reports back to Washington, D. C. Often he was too sick to dictate them to a secretary. Irving considered resigning, but with the Spanish government so uncertain, both he and Secretary of State Webster thought the timing was unwise.

Finally, Irving assumed a leadership role. Whether Espartero or Narváez were to be in charge of the Spanish government was not of concern to the United States. Diplomatic relations could go on with either of the men. What concerned Irving was the safety of a twelve-year-old girl. No harm should come

Irving assisted twelve-year-old Queen Isabella II during the Spanish Revolution of 1843.

to Queen Isabella. Irving sent out letters to all the foreign diplomats in Madrid to join him at the royal palace if the rebel army should take over the city. They would then stand firm to protect the monarch.

It was a brave offer. It appeared to Irving that blood might be shed if there were a direct confrontation between the Espartero and Narváez forces. Some might be reluctant to kill a young girl, but killing grown men who were judged to be interfering with the internal matters of their country—that might be different. Nonetheless, the diplomats voiced their willingness to support Irving's offer.

Irving was surprised to receive the answer he did from the royal palace. The queen "respectfully declined" the offer extended by the diplomats in Madrid. As it turned out, Isabella was working directly with the rebel forces led by Narváez. There was no final showcase between the opposing forces. Espartero left Spain quietly and quickly, making his way to a safe refuge in England.

Although busy with his diplomatic post and fighting off illness as well, Irving's desire to write remained strong. In April 1846, Washington Irving resigned his position as foreign minister to Spain.

As he descended the ship *Cambriar* in the Boston Harbor on September 18, 1846, Irving knew he had made the correct decision to return to the United States. He was greeted by family and friends eager to welcome him home. At sixty-three, he enjoyed the reputation of being America's best known writer.

"Should this be a country where crowns be presented to those who have achieved grand and noble accomplishment, Washington Irving would be wearing one of the finest gold," wrote one newspaper editor. "It is a joyful occasion to welcome him back to his home soil. Let us all hope, selfish as it be, that this master of words has many more of them to share with his waiting readers."

Chapter Seven

Sunnyside

For many years he had wanted to write a biography about that American hero he had met so long ago and whose name he shared, George Washington. He had also started a biography about Oliver Goldsmith, the famous British poet. The religious figure, Mahomet, also interested Irving as a biographical subject. In a letter to a friend, Irving wrote:

"In the early part of my literary career I used to think I would take warning by the fate of writers who worked until they 'wrote themselves down,' and that I would retire while still in the freshness of my powers, but you see circumstances have obliged me to change my plan and I am likely to write on until the pen drops from my hand."

Those "circumstances" revolved around money. Irving constantly feared not being able pay his bills. He had learned to enjoy the finer things in life such as stylish clothes, good food and beverage, and attending fancy parties. Now into his sixties and still a bachelor, he worried about not having anyone to take care of him as he grew older.

Once safely and comfortably returned to Sunnyside, Irving

picked up his pen. Not only was he eager to write, he also needed to raise money. His brother, Ebenezer, a widower with five daughters, seemed unable to keep himself afloat financially. Irving was always willing to assist in family matters and welcomed the group to Sunnyside. The girls repaid their Uncle Irving with constant love and affection.

Pierre Munro Irving, Washington's nephew, provided his uncle with secretarial skills and budgeting assistance. Pierre kept a careful eye on his Uncle Washington. Someday, he planned to write a biography about him. In addition to the care he took to protect his uncle from exhausting himself with work, guests, and speaking engagements, Pierre recorded many personal notes for his own future writing project.

Although Washington Irving planned to dedicate himself to his writing projects now that he was back at Sunnyside, he was definitely not going to work all the time. During his lifetime, he had found much pleasure in social activities. He was a delightful storyteller. He still enjoyed a fine meal accompanied by a good glass of wine. Whether the guests be at one of his Sunnyside gatherings or whether he was attending a relative's or a friend's party, Irving could be counted on to provide pleasurable conversation.

Irving finished projects he had put on hold; *The Life of Oliver Goldsmith* appeared in 1846 and *Mahomet and His Successors* in 1850. Then he plunged into the writing of the life of George Washington. Previous biographies had made the country's Revolutionary War leader and first president without flaws, a godlike creation who did not converse but rather gave speeches, who knew no fear, and never had an unkind thought. Irving set out to write a true account of an extraordinary man, a man who had weaknesses as well as virtue. "There was no need to embellish George Washington; his life was worthy of great admiration," Irving asserted. "Yet he was a human being, who reached within himself and molded leadership on the field of battle and in the realm of government. We would hope others might follow his example, but this will not be accomplished if this man be lifted beyond the reach and understanding of ordinary people."

Irving compiled information about the man for whom he was named. This was a manuscript Irving wanted to be perfect. The subject was a hero to the nation and deserved the best. Not only that, but he was growing tired. Irving was now in his seventies, and the work on the biography took much of his energy. He had begun to slow down.

In 1855, five years after Irving had begun, the first volume of his biography about George Washington was published. One newspaper heralded the news with the headline: "WASHINGTON by WASHINGTON." Readers applauded the book, urging Irving to produce the second volume immediately. The response cheered Irving, pushing him forward with his writing. Within months, he produced the second volume. Once again, people responded with delight. William Hickling Prescott, a longtime admirer and Spanish historian, wrote: "You have done with Washington just as I thought you would, and, instead of a cold marble statue of a demi-god, you have made him a being of flesh and blood, like ourselves—one with

Irving completed his last work, a biography of George Washington, at Sunnyside.

whom we can have sympathy. The general sentiment of the country has been too decidedly expressed for you to doubt for a moment that this is the portrait of him which is to hold a permanent place in the national gallery."

Once again, the glowing reception of his work pleased Irving. Yet it could not hold off the aches and pains he was suffering. Irving knew time was running out. He fought to sleep at nights, and during the daytime sneezing and coughing spells from asthma weakened him. On April 3, 1858, family and friends gathered to observe his seventy-fifth birthday. Clearly, Irving was aging. "I do not fear death," he declared, "but I would like to go down with all sails set."

Finishing the biography of George Washington remained his final goal. His nephew Pierre insisted on frequent doctor visits in New York City until, finally, Washington moved there in the winter of 1858-59. His physical ailments were compounded by his nervousness. He had to finish this last project.

On March 15, 1859, the job was done. In total, the book ran five volumes. Extra efforts were made to have the complete biographical set in Irving's hands by his seventy-sixth birthday. The book had been first envisioned thirty years before, and now he called it "the last labor of my pen."

Naturally, Irving was delighted when critics hailed his Washington biography as "magnificent" and "superb." But when a friend declared that he had read parts of the book to his children and they liked it, Irving considered it ultimate praise.

At the end of his life Irving preferred to stay at home with his family and friends.

"That's it; that is what I write it for," said Irving. "I want it so clear that anybody can understand it. I want the action to shine through the style. No style, indeed; no encumbrance of ornament..."

His writing finished, Washington Irving took to other pursuits. Carefully he put his diaries and notebooks together and presented them to his nephew Pierre. "Someone will be writing my life when I am gone, and I wish you to do it." The younger Irving took notes constantly at Sunnyside, keeping a close watch over his uncle's health. Yes, he would write his uncle's story, and it would be accurate.

Irving busied himself as much as he could, visiting family and friends, amazing many of them with his alert memory. Always skilled at playing cards, he continued to emerge the winner at regular sessions of whist at the table. The Christ Church in Tarrytown regularly found him at the vestry meetings.

Sunnyside guests found their host to be "mentally alert" and of "good humor." One visitor, obviously shocked at Irving's vitality, openly remarked how well Irving looked and acted. The answer came back: "You would have me giving way to my years? Time is not to be wasted. For those kind enough to stay with me a while should not have to face a confused fool."

Another guest, an editor of the *New York Independent*, called on Irving in November of 1859. He asked the writer which of his literary works he looked back on with greatest pleasure. Irving shook his head. "If I had another twenty years

Irving's nephew Pierre Munro published a four-volume biography about his uncle in 1863.

of life," he said, "I should rewrite every one of them." More often, he seemed to talk with pride and pleasure at what he had written.

He passed his final days at Sunnyside. "My own place has never been so beautiful as at present," he wrote in a diary. "I have made more openings by pruning and cutting down trees, so that from the piazza I have several charming views of the Tappan Zee and the hills beyond, all set, as it were, in verdant frames; and I am never tired of sitting there in my old Voltaire chair, of a long summer morning, with a book in my hand, sometimes reading, sometimes musing, and sometimes dozing, and mixing all up in a pleasant dream."

On Monday, November 28, 1859, Washington Irving walked around the grounds of his beloved Sunnyside. By afternoon, he showed the exhaustion of his exercise by his heavy breathing. Yet that evening he ate a full meal and remarked over the beauty of the sunset that filled the dining room. When a niece went to see that he was ready for bed, Irving clutched his side and collapsed on the floor. His nephew Pierre hurried to him and a doctor was summoned. There was nothing anyone could do.

The news of Washington Irving's death saddened people in all parts of the world. Not only had his writing entertained countless readers, other famous authors had been influenced by his work. Edgar Allen Poe, Nathaniel Hawthorne, Ralph Waldo Emerson, Herman Melville, and Henry Wadsworth Longfellow—all major American writers—gave credit to Irving and his work for helping them create quality literature.

Across the sea, Charles Dickens and William Thackeray did the same.

Washington Irving was laid to rest with other family members in Tarrytown's Sleepy Hollow Cemetery. The marker on his gravesite is simple: "Washington Irving, son of William and Sarah S. Irving, was seventy-six years, seven months, and twenty-five days old when he died November 28, 1859."

The words are few for one who gave the world so many.

Major Works

1802-03	*Letters of Jonathan Oldstyle, Gent.*
1807-08	*Salmagundi*
1809	*Knickerbocker's History of New York*
1819-20	*The Sketch Book*
1822	*Bracebridge Hall*
1824	*Tales of a Traveler*
1828	*The Life and Voyages of Christopher Columbus*
1829	*The Conquest of Granada*
1831	*Voyages and Discoveries of the Companions of Columbus*
1832	*The Alhambra*
1835	"A Tour on the Praires" included in *The Crayon Miscellany*
1836	*Astoria*
1837	*The Adventures of Captain Bonneville*

1840	*The Life of Oliver Goldsmith, with Selections from his Writings*
1841	*Biography and Poetical Remains of the Late Margaret Miller Davidson*
1849	*The Life of Oliver Goldsmith*, revised
1850	*Mahomet and His Successors*
1855	*Wolfert's Roost*
1855-59	*Life of George Washington*

Timeline

1783 —born April 3 in New York City.

1793 —begins studying law.

1802 —publishes *Letters of Jonathan Oldstyle, Gent.*

1804-06—visits Europe.

1807-08—publishes *Salmagundi* with brother William and James Kirke Paulding.

1809 —Matilda Hoffman dies.

—publishes *Diedrich Knickenbocker's History of New York.*

1813-14—edits *Analetic* magazine.

1814 —serves as military aid to New York governor.

1815 —sails to England.

1819-20—publishes *The Sketch Book.*

1822 —publishes *Bracebridge Hall.*

1822-23—lives in Dresden, Germany.

1824 —publishes *Tales of a Traveler.*

1826-29—lives in Madrid, Spain as attache to American legation.

1828 —publishes *The Life and Voyages of Christopher Columbus.*

1829 —publishes *A Chronicle of the Conquest of Granada.*

1829-31—lives in London, England, as secretary of American legation.

1832   —publishes *The Alhambra.*
        —returns to the United States.
1835   —publishes "A Tour on The Prairies".
        —buys Sunnyside.
1836   —publishes *Astoria.*
1837   —publishes *The Adventures of Captain Bonneville.*
1842-46—serves as American foreign minister to Spain.
1849   —publishes *Oliver Goldsmith.*
1849-50—publishes *Mahomet and His Successors.*
1855-59—publishes *The Life of George Washington.*
1859   —dies November 28 at Sunnyside.

Bibliography

Benet, Laura, *Washington Irving*. New York: Dodd, Mead & Company, 1944.

Bolton, Sarah K., *Famous American Authors*. New York: Thomas J.Crowell Company, 1954.

Bowden, Mary Weatherspoon, *Washington Irving*. Boston: Twayne Publishers, 1981.

Brooks, Van Wyck, *The World of Washington Irving*. New York: E. P Dutton & Company, 1950.

Hancock, Carla, *Seven Founders of American Literature*. Winston-Salem, North Carolina: John F. Blair, 1976.

Hedges, William L. *Washington Irving: An American Study, 1802-1832*. Baltimore: John Hopkins Press, 1965.

Hellman, George Sidney, *Washington Irving, Esquire*. New York: Alfred A. Knolf, 1925.

Irving, Washington, *The Complete Works of Washington Irving: Journals and Notebooks*. ed. Nathalia Wright. vol I&IV, Madison: University of Wisconsin Press, 1969.

McFarland, Philip. *Sojourners*. New York: Antheneum, 1979.

Peare, Catherine Owens, *Washington Irving—His Life*. New York: Henry Holt and Company, 1957.

Seton, Anya, *Washington Irving*. Boston: Houghton Mifflin Company, 1960.

Williams, Stanley T., *The Life of Washington Irving*. New York: Oxford University Press, 1935.

Wood, James P., *A Life of Washington Irving*. New York: Pantheon Books, 1967.

Sources

CHAPTER ONE

p. 10, "Let us call the child Washington...." adapted from Williams, Stanley T., *The Life of Washington Irving*. New York: Oxford Un. Press, 1935, p. 3.

p. 12, "Your excellency....Here's a bairn that's called after ye!" Williams, p. 10.

CHAPTER TWO

p. 20, "a dismembered branch of the Appalachian family..." McFarland, Philip, *Sojourners*. New York: Atheneum, 1979, p. 152.

p. 22, "In several parts of the road I have been up to my middle in mud and water...." Irving, Washington, *The Complete Works of Washington Irving: Journals and Notebooks*. ed. Nathalia Wright. vol. I, University of Wisconsin Press: Madison, 1969, p. 16.

p. 22, "The Sovereign Dirt erects her Throne...", ibid., p. 16.

p. 22, "...the most impudent, chattering, forward scoundrel," ibid., p. 22.

p. 22 "I never passed so dreary a night in my life...."ibid., p. 23.

p. 24, "Their dark complexions, rough beards, and fierce black eyes scowling under enormous bushy eyebrows...." ibid., p. 149.

p. 28, "to instruct the young, inform the old, correct the town, and castigate the age." Williams, p. 80.

p. 32, "...absolutely enchanted with Richmond," McFarland, p. 74.

p. 32, "May his treachery to his country exalt him..." McFarland, p. 78.

p. 33, "treason was never intended by Burr." McFarland, p. 78.

CHAPTER THREE

p. 35, "She died in the flower of her youth and of mine but she has lived for me ever since in all woman kind...."Williams, p. 104.

p. 36, SIR, Having read in your paper of the 26th October last...." Williams, p. 112.

p. 39, "I beg you to accept my best thanks for the uncommon degree of entertainment which I have received from the most excellent...." McFarland, p. 107.

p. 51, "I felt the value of life and health now in a degree that I never did before...." Williams, p. 222.

CHAPTER FOUR

p. 52, "In Dresden I have a very neat, comfortable, and prettily furnished apartment...." McFarland, p. 209.

p. 58, "Breakfast. coffee and milk excellent bread. Drive all day thro a wild mountainous...." Washington, Irving. *The Complete Works of Washington Irving*. ed. Nathalia Wright. vol. IV, Madison: University of Wisconsin Press, 1969, p. 7.

p. 58, "arrive for the night at hotel at village of Lerma...." ibid., p. 7.

p. 64, "I have always admired your work." McFarland, p. 315.

p. 65, "I am so in love with this apartment that I can hardly force myself from it..." Williams, p. 367.

CHAPTER FIVE

p. 70, "I'm asked how long I mean to stay here...." Bolton, Sarah K., *Famous American Authors*. New York: Thomas J. Crowell Company, 1954, p. 13.

p. 72, "clearings on the banks of the rivers...a solitary log hut with corn fields among the forests." McFarland, p. 431.

CHAPTER SIX

p. 82, "Charles Dickens, guest of the nation!" McFarland, p. 357.

CHAPTER SEVEN

p. 92, "You have done with Washington just as I thought you would...." McFarland, p. 494.

p. 96, "That's it; that's what I write for...." Bowden, Mary Weatherspoon, *Washington Irving.* Boston: Twayne Publishers, 1981, p.182.

Index

The Adventures of Captain Bonneville, 73
The Alhambra, 70, 74
American Revolution, 9-10, 16-17, 45, 50, 68, 91
Analectic, 40
Astor, John Jacob, 73, 75
Astoria, 73-74

Bonaparte, Napoleon, 30
Bonneville, Benjamin, 73-74
Bracebridge Hall, 48
Bunyan, John, 11
Burr, Aaron, 30-33

Chaucer, Geoffrey, 11
Columbia College, 16
Columbus, Christopher, 56-58, 60-62, 64

Dickens, Charles, 82-84, 99
Dolgorouki, Dimitri, Prince of Russia, 64

Edinburgh Review, 48
Ellsworth, Henry, 70

Emerson, Ralph Waldo, 98
Espartero, Baldomero, 85-86, 88
Everett, Alexander, 56-57, 60

Ferdinand II, King of Aragon, 57
Foster, Emily, 53, 55, 58
Foster, Flora, 53, 55
Frederick Augustus I, King of Germany, 51

Goldsmith, Oliver, 90, 91

Hamilton, Alexander, 30
Harrison, William Henry, 78, 80
Hawthorne, Nathaniel, 98
Hell Gate, 73
A History of New York from the Beginning of the World to the End of the Dutch Dynasty, 36-39, 41, 43-44
A History of the Life and Voyages of Christopher Columbus, 64
Hoffman, Josiah, 21, 23-24, 26
Hoffman, Matilda, 24-26, 28, 33-35, 44, 53

Irving, Anne, 9, 11, 14, 18-19, 33
Irving, Catherine, 9, 11, 14, 18-19, 33
Irving, Ebenezer, (brother) 9, 11, 14, 16, 23, 33, 91
Irving, Ebenezer, (uncle) 10, 14
Irving, John, (brother) 9, 11, 14, 16-17, 23, 26, 33
Irving, Peter, 9, 11, 14, 16-17, 23, 33, 35, 39-41, 50, 53, 56-60, 64
Irving, Pierre Munro, 73, 91, 94, 96-98
Irving, Sarah, (mother) 9-11, 33, 41, 99
Irving, Sarah, (sister) 9, 11, 14, 33, 41-42, 60, 68
Irving, Washington,
    and Aaron Burr trial, 30-33
    visits American West, 70, 72
    as businessman, 21, 39-42, 48
    visits Canada, 21-23
    childhood, 9-14
    criticism of, 39, 48, 54, 56, 64, 70, 74, 78, 89, 92, 94
    death, 98
    as diplomat, 67-69, 80, 82, 84-86, 88
    education, 11-12, 14-16, 23-24, 26
    visits England, 40-42, 68-69, 84
    visits France, 23-24, 53, 56, 84
    visits Germany, 51-53
    and illness, 50, 86, 92, 94
    and journalism, 17-18, 26, 28, 36, 38, 40
    as lawyer, 16-18, 21, 23-24, 26, 28, 30, 35, 67
    legacy, 98-99
    and love affairs, 24, 26, 33-35, 53
    visits Spain, 56-58, 60, 62, 64-68, 82
    as translator, 56-57, 60
    visits upstate New York, 19-21
    as Whig, 78-79
Irving, William Sr., 9-11, 14, 16-17, 19-20, 33, 41, 99
Irving, William, (uncle) 10, 14
Irving, William, (brother) 9, 11, 14, 16, 23, 26-28, 33, 50
Isabella I, Queen of Castile, 57
Isabella II, Queen of Spain, 85-88

Jefferson, Thomas, 30, 32
Jeffrey, Francis, 48

Kilmaster, Ann, 11

LaTrobe, Charles, 70
"The Legend of Sleepy Hollow," 46-48
"The Letters of Jonathan Oldstyle, Gent.," 17
The Life of Oliver Goldsmith, 91
The Life of Washington, 92, 94
Livingston, Henry Brockholst, 16

Longfellow, Henry Wadsworth, 63-64, 76, 98
Longworth, David, 28
Mahomet and His Successors, 91
Mahomet, 90
Marshall, John, 32
Melville, Herman, 98
Molina, Antonia, 65
Morning Chronicle, 17

Narváez, Ramón María, 85-86, 88
de Navarrete, Martin Fernandez, 56-57, 60
New York Evening Post, 36, 38
New York Independent, 96

P. Irving and Company, 10, 36, 39-42, 48
Pacific Fur Company, 73, 75
Paulding, James Kirke, 17, 26-28
Pilgrim's Progress, 11
Poe, Edgar Allan, 98
Pourtalès, Count Albert-Alexandre, 70
Prescott, William Hickling, 92

Rich, Obadiah, 57, 59
"Rip Van Winkle," 44-46, 49
Romaine, Benjamin, 15

Salmagundi, 26-28

Scott, Sir Walter, 39, 42-43, 50-51
"Scottish Lizzie," 12-14
Shakespeare, William, 11
The Sketch-Book of Geoffrey Crayon, Gent., 44, 48, 50, 64, 74
Southern Literary Messenger, 76
Spanish Revolution, 85-87
Sunnyside, 76-78, 80, 90-91, 93, 95-96, 98

Tales of a Traveler, 54, 64
Thackeray, William, 99
Tompkins, Daniel, 40
"A Tour on the Prairies," 72

Washington, George, 10, 12-14, 90-94
Webster, Daniel, 79, 81
Wilkie, Sir David, 60, 62, 64-65
Wilkinson, James, 33
The World Displayed, 14